MEDITATIONS
WITH™
NATIVE AMERICANS —
LAKOTA SPIRITUALITY

Introduction and versions by
PAUL B. STEINMETZ, S.J.

Foreword by
ÅKE HULTKRANTZ

Bear & C
Santa Fe, New Mexico

1

Bear & Company Books are published by Bear & Company, Inc. Its Trademark, consisting of the words "Bear & Company" and the portrayal of a bear, is Registered in U.S. Patent and Trademark Office and in other countries. Marca Registrada Bear & Company, Inc. Drawer 2860, Santa Fe, New Mexico 87504. PRINTED IN THE UNITED STATES OF AMERICA

Meditations with™ and the representation thereof, is registered in U.S. Patent and Trademark Office and in other countries, Marca Registrada, Bear & Company, Inc., Drawer 2860, Santa Fe, New Mexico 87504.

Bear & Company, Inc.
P.O. Drawer 2860
Santa Fe, NM 87504

Cover art & line illustrations — Martin Red Bear

Table of Contents

WHAT IS THE MEDITATIONS WITH ™ SERIES?

Bear & Co. is publishing this series of creation-centered mystic/prophets to bring to the attention and prayer of peoples today the power and energy of the holistic mystics of the western tradition. One reason western culture succumbs to boredom and to violence is that we are not being challenged by our religious traditions to be all we can be. This is also the reason that many sincere spiritual seekers go East for their mysticism — because the West is itself out of touch with its deepest spiritual guides. The format Bear & Co. has chosen in which to present these holistic mystic/prophets is deliberate: We do not feel that more academically-styled books on our mystics is what every-day believers need: Rather, we wish to get the mystics of personal and social transformation off our dusty shelves and into the hearts and minds and bodies of our people. To do this we choose a format that is ideal for meditation, for imaging, for sharing in groups and in prayer occasions. We rely on primary sources for the texts but we let the author's words and images flow from her or his inner structure to our deep inner selves.

Foreword

The author of this book of meditations is a remarkable man, out of the ordinary, and occupies a unique position in American Indian religious studies.

For a couple of decades Father Paul Steinmetz, S.J., served as a dedicated missionary among the Oglala Lakota in South Dakota. It was during this time that he launched the startling Christian reinterpretation of Lakota religion based upon the inspiration that the sacred pipe, the most holy of Lakota religious sacramentals, could be transformed into a symbol of Christ. Not unexpectedly this innovation in ritual theology created mostly favorable reactions among the Indians concerned, served as a model of missionary adaptation and provoked an engaging debate among anthropologists. It was also during this time that Paul Steinmetz himself took on the role of the anthropologist and conducted field research among the Oglala — with great reward, for the Oglala evidently put much trust in him. So Father Paul finally turned out as both a missionary and a scholar in the anthropology of religion, a subject in which he finally earned his Ph.D. As a man of high intellectual ability and deep human kindness, he has managed to make weighty achievements in both these activities.

His connections with American Indian religion are two-dimensional. I know of no other person in modern times who, to the same extent, has been both a subject in and an object of scholarly research on North American Indian religion. He has engaged himself deeply in such research, but he is also himself part and parcel of recent native American religious history.

It is only natural that with this background Paul Steinmetz has come close to the hearts of a great many Lakota Indians. He knows their situation today, their difficult adjustment to two worlds, Indian and white, and their zest for the religious mystery. As in Beatrice Weasel Bear's intimate statement, the Lakota feels himself linked to all the major forms of religion he finds on his Reservation, be they traditional Indian, Christian or Peyote. There is here an amazing sense of the unity of religion, of a religious fellowship behind the structuring of symbols. Father Paul is convinced that all these religious forms find a true interpretation in the light of the Christian Gospel, and that Lakota spirituality may enrich the religious life of modern man. The

5

statements by Indians that he communicates certainly convey the impression that the distance between the religions is very small on the level of personal meditation. Whatever our reaction, we perceive that in a congenial way Father Paul has been in touch with the deepest flow of emotions in American Indian spirituality.

This is a thought-provoking book, a book to have and to cherish.

Dr. Ake Hultkrantz
University of Sweden
Stockholm

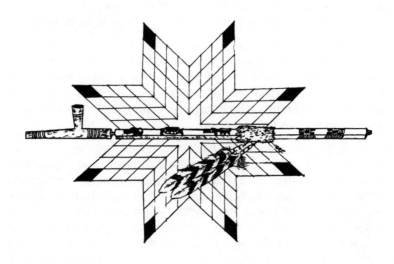

Acknowledgments

I am indebted to many Lakota, both living and dead, for the privilege of sharing these meditations with you. John Iron Rope, a Catholic medicine man, gave his approval when I prayed with the Sacred Pipe at the funeral of Red Long Visitor. This was the beginning of many beautiful friendships.

Frank Fools Crow, the leader of the tribal Sun Dance for many years, was delighted that a Catholic priest prayed with the Sacred Pipe. George Plenty Wolf was a medicine man who brought his Lakota and Christian beliefs together. Pete Catches, Sr., formally a Catholic catechist, was my spiritual director on my Vision Quest. I formed friendships with Charles Kills Rhee, Dawson No Horse and Richard Moves Camp, all medicine men. Selo Black Crow is a Lakota spiritual leader who conducts his own Sun Dance on the reservation. Edgar Red Cloud was the great grandson of Chief Red Cloud and head Sun Dance singer for many years. Lucy Looks Twice was a living link to the famous Black Elk about whom John Neihardt and Joseph Epes Brown wrote. Lawrence Hunter introduced me to Stanley Looking Horse who helps his son, Orval, as keeper of the Sacred Calf Pipe.

Beatrice Weasel Bear, daughter of Rex Long Visitor, introduced me into the Native American Church. Her husband, John, was a road man, one who conducts Peyote meetings. She considers me a member of her family. She gave me valuable insights on bringing together the Sacred Pipe and the Peyote traditions. She also sponsored a Peyote meeting for me on my journey to Europe and again on my return.

Emerson Spider, as State High Priest for the Native American Church in South Dakota, speaks with authority. Bernard Ice was blind and most delighted that his spiritual vision was being recorded for the benefit of others. Bernard Red Cloud, also a descendant of the Chief, and his wife Christine are important members of the church. Lawrence Hunter told me about the early days of Peyote on the Pine Ridge Reservation from his own personal experience.

These and other Lakota shared their spirituality with me and enriched my life.

Preface

Native American Spirituality is a part of Technological Man, a part of himself which he has repressed into his unconscious. It is for this reason that Native Americans can help Technological Man get in touch with his own primal roots. This is the only way he will redeem the world of nature which he has been exploiting and polluting. No program nor plan will accomplish this. It must be a spirituality that expresses a personal relationship with nature. From this personal relationship flow a love and respect towards nature, a willingness not to dominate but to be a part of nature and an ability to view creation sacramentally. But Technological Man must not only bring up this spirituality from his own primal unconscious, he must also assimilate the contents into his own conscious life, a process Carl Jung called individuation. Since his tradition is a Christian one, this assimilation results in a Native American Christian Spirituality. Time is running out. There is a sense of urgency. This spirituality is not a luxury but a necessity.

The religious experiences expressed in this book are presented as meditations to help one develop a Native American Christian Spirituality, or more precisely, a Lakota Christian Spirituality. Therefore, this book is intended not only to be read but to be used for *meditation*. It was an amazing experience for me to discover how much arranging the material from my doctoral dissertation into sense lines encouraged meditation rather than mere reading. The spirituality shared with me personally by the Lakota is so rich in religious symbols that it requires a leisurely journey in the imagination to allow the symbols to speak to the heart. Marie Louise von Franz in commenting on the nature of symbolism writes:

> A still living symbol can never be "resolved" (that is analyzed, understood) by a rational interpretation, but can only be circumscribed and amplified by conscious associations; its nucleus, which is pregnant with meaning, remains unconscious as long as it is living and can only be divined. If one interprets it intellectually, one "kills" the symbol, thus preventing any further unfolding of its content...The more significantly a symbol expresses an unconscious component that is common to a large number of people, the greater its effect on society.[1]

This book, then, is intended as a psychological amplification of Lakota Spirituality since it is with them that I have intimate experience. Its purpose is to lead the reader through a rich association of symbols to an intuitive insight into Lakota religious experience and to touch his or her unconscious depths to evoke one's own personal symbols. Consequently, I am letting this experience speak for itself without analysis and with a minimum of introductory material.

We are, indeed, dealing with the symbols that express the unconscious depths of Native American people. They are sharing their innermost feelings with us and we should approach them with respect, reverence, and gratitude. And so, we meditate with the Native Americans and not on them.

Paul B. Steinmetz, S.J.
St. Gerard Majella Church
Los Angeles, California

Introduction

A brief background on Lakota identity and on the principal elements of their spirituality will help one better appreciate and understand these meditations.

The Lakota Indians

The Teton Tribe speaking Lakota is one of the seven Sioux Tribes, two of the others speaking the dialect of Nakota and four that of Dakota. The Oglala is a sub-tribe of the Teton Lakota. The word "Sioux," which was applied to all seven tribes, is a French corruption of an Algonquin word meaning "adder," that is, enemy. The Sioux were first mentioned by white explorers around 1640 in the western Great Lake Region. They lived off hunting, fishing and the gathering of lake and forest products. Partly due to the pressure from the Ojibwa or Chippewa, the Lakota branch moved westward into the northern plains in the early 1700's and filtered into the Black Hills sometime after 1750. During this time they acquired the horse and became the well known buffalo hunters and warbonnett warriors. This way of life lasted for the Oglala until they were confined to the Pine Ridge Reservation in South Dakota in 1878. Red Cloud, who successfully defeated the U.S. Army in all his battles, became the chief of the Oglala Lakota and led his people in their political struggles. In 1890 the excitement generated by the Ghost Dance Religion resulted in the Wounded Knee Massacre, an event which ended active resistance against the U.S. Government.

Traditional Lakota Spirituality

The Sacred Calf Pipe. The Sacred Pipe was common to all the Plains tribes. However, each tribe has its own religious tradition which gives a unique meaning to the Sacred Pipe. Of these the best known tradition is the Lakota myth of the Woman bringing the Buffalo Calf Pipe as Black Elk related it to Joseph Epes Brown in the late 1940's on the Pine Ridge Reservation.

In a time of famine, two hunters saw a beautiful woman coming from a distance. One hunter, who had evil desires towards her, was reduced to a skeleton. The woman told the other hunter to prepare the people for her return. A lodge was made from several tipis and the people were all excited. Suddenly she appeared, entered the lodge, presented Chief Standing Hollow Horn with a Pipe and told him that their prayers through the Pipe would always be answered and that seven religious ceremonies (sweat lodge, vision quest, making of relatives, keeping of the soul, girl's puberty rite, the sundance, and the throwing the ball rite) would be given them. According to Lakota mythology it is believed that at the beginning of the cycle a buffalo loses one hair, and every age he loses one leg. When all his hair and all four legs are gone, then the waters rush in once again and the circle comes to an end. Some believe that today the buffalo is on his last leg.

What is regarded as the original Calf Pipe is kept at Green Grass on the Cheyenne River Reservation in South Dakota. There has been a continuous line of keepers, the present one being Orval Looking Horse, who is in his twenties. Green Grass has become a place of pilgrimage. Medicine men and Indian activists from many tribes have been going there. An impressive Sun Dance is held there every year, drawing from many tribes. Green Grass is the center of the Lakota religious world and becoming more pan-Indian.

Relationship to the Earth and the Spirit World. Lakota Spirituality relates one both to the world of visible creation and to the world of spirits. It forms in us a personal relationship to the Earth so that we treat her with respect and reverence. It is a centering of ourselves in creation through a relationship to the four directions, the foundations of the universe and the place where spirits dwell. Through this spirituality we learn to live in harmony with all creatures. It also puts us at ease with the spirits through accepting their presence and through the offering of spiritual food.

Spiritual Food. Food becomes a sacramental sign when it is offered on behalf of the spirits of the deceased. It is called spiritual food because it has a purpose beyond feeding our bodies. Through this symbolic offering one brings blessings to deceased relatives and friends.

The Sweat Lodge Ceremony. The sweat lodge ceremony was practiced throughout the entire North American continent probably for thousands of years. The sweat lodge is a dome-shaped structure about four feet high, formed by bent willow saplings and covered with canvas or blankets. The door faces the east, the direction of the morning star and the rising sun which are symbols of renewal. During the ceremony hot rocks are placed in a central hole and cold water is poured over them to create intense heat. It is not only a purification rite; it is also a prayer ceremony in which we offer up prayers through suffering and is a means of establishing a proper relationship between the sacred and the profane worlds.

The Vision Quest. One medicine man called this ceremony the Pipe Fast since it has purposes other than seeking a vision. However, the vision is its highest expression. Young men, beginning in their teens, and medicine men commonly go on a Vision Quest, although men and women of most ages also undergo the experience. The person, alone, fasts from both food and water for up to four days on a hill within a sacred place, marked off by the colored flags of the four directions and a string of tiny tobacco pouches stretched out between them. Visions are the source of power needed to perform religious ceremonies praying with the Pipe through the intercession of the spirits. The experience is very much like being ordained a priest or minister in one of the Christian traditions. Visions and dreams, closely related, give us a rich source of religious symbols.

The Sun Dance. The Sun Dance was a ceremony common to most of the Plains tribes. It was the only time in the year when the entire tribe gathered together. In the past, it was held in June when there was a plentiful supply of grass and buffalo meat. Modern supplies have allowed it to be moved to July and August. Sun Dance ceremonies were impressive ceremonies of tribal unity and renewal in which Plains Indians fulfilled their personal vows of thanksgiving. The men dancers were pierced either in the chest and tied to the cottonwood tree or in the back to drag buffalo skulls. The woman dancers made flesh offerings.

Today, goals that are more psychological, such as seeking one's identity, have developed. In addition, there are multiple Sun Dances on a reservation, as many as eight one summer on the Pine Ridge Reservation. However, it is still the most intense moment of spirituality among the Plains Indians and evokes a sense of renewal and dedication. Men and women fast and dance for four days, the men being pierced and the women making flesh offerings.

Yuwipi Meetings. Healing ceremonies conducted by medicine men are common to all the Plains tribes. Among the Lakota they are called *yuwipi*, "to bind up." The *yuwipi* man prays through the spirits acquired in the vision quest. In the full *yuwipi* meeting the *yuwipi* man, with his hands tied behind his back, is tied inside a blanket and laid on the floor amidst a congregation of around twenty-five men, women, and children. Lights are extinguished and one hears the *yuwipi* man praying in a muffled voice in total darkness. His power is validated by the belief that the spirits untie him. Towards the end of the meeting he has been freed and he prays in a clear voice. Practice of *yuwipi* greatly increased during the reservation period among the

Lakota since it gave a sense of power to the powerless. The practice of *yuwipi* evokes genuine religious symbols that give valuable insights into the nature of religious power, even though there are still unanswered questions on the presence and activities of the spirits.

The Native American Church.

The Native American Church is a pan-Indian tradition which diffused from Oklahoma throughout most of the Plains Indian tribes, beginning in 1870. It came to the Pine Ridge Reservation around 1904. The members use Peyote, a mild hallucinogenic, as a sacrament. Offering a new way of acquiring visions other than the Vision Quest is one of the dynamics of the Native American Church.

Peyote meetings are the center of the religion. They last about twelve hours, from sunset to beyond sunrise. There are two different fireplaces, the Half Moon and the Cross Fire, so named because these designs are part of the altar. The Half Moon on the Pine Ridge Reservation includes some traditional Lakota symbols and the Cross Fire is more explicitly Christian. There are four officials in a meeting: the one who conducts it, called a road man in the Half Moon and a minister in the Cross Fire; the main drummer; the cedar man; and the fire man. The road man or minister states the purpose of the meeting—funeral, memorial, birthday, back to school, thanksgiving, or occasionally healing. However, people are prayed over during all types of meetings. Then he cedars the instruments, which include the water drum, the staff, feathered fan, and gourd rattle along with the Chief Peyote which is placed on the altar. The road man then offers the opening prayer (in the Half Moon the ceremonial cigarette is used during this and three other prayers) and sings the four opening songs. After this, the instruments are passed around the entire group for anyone who wants to sing. This continues until the midnight water call, when the fire man talks, prays, and blesses the water which is passed around for everyone to drink. Then the drumming and singing continues until early morning when the sponsor of the meeting talks, prays, and blesses water. The singing then continues. At sunrise the meeting reaches a climax when the morning water woman brings in the ceremonial breakfast of water, corn, meat, and fruit. She talks and prays, during which time she always cries. The breakfast is passed around from person to person, each one drinking from the same cup and eating from the same bowl. With this, the meeting is concluded. There is a large dinner around noon before which water is blessed for the fourth time. Everyone drinks the blessed water before eating.

The Native American Church creates a strong sense of community which is very supportive. To walk the Peyote Road is this Church's way of saying to live a good moral life. Important elements of the Native American Church are:

The Altar. The altar is the most sacred space in a meeting. The Chief Peyote sits upon the altar. It contains the fireplace. Especially in a tipi meeting, gazing into the fire is a source of centering and concentration. As we shall see, the altar evokes many rich symbols. Bernard Ice's remarks on the altar have a poignant meaning since he was blind.

The Water Drum. The drum is the heart beat of religious celebration throughout the entire primal world. One must experience its steady rhythmic beat to understand its impact on the primal imagination. The fast-changing beat of the water drum during the long night of a Peyote meeting evokes a rich religious experience.

The Morning Water Woman. The Morning Water Woman takes the same place as Mother Earth in the traditional Lakota Spirituality. She has an emotional appeal and touches the hearts of all those who have gone through a long night of praying and singing.

Peyote Visions. The hallucinogenic effect of Peyote can be over-emphasized. Although it does facilitate visions, other factors such as gazing into the fire, the hypnotic beat of the drum, and the sense of concentration felt in the group are also factors. The attitude of regarding the Peyote as a sacrament deepens the experience. Peyote visions are important.

Eschatological Reflections. Members of the Native American Church have the ability to reflect upon the end of the world as a fulfillment of their religious tradition. It is a goal not only to be accepted but even desired and sought for.

Christian Influences

Early Christian missionaries failed to appreciate the value of Lakota Indian Spirituality. However, the Lakota, at least, began to understand their spirituality through Christian values. In recent years, the first steps have been taken in the Lakota imagination towards a Lakota Christian Spirituality. This fulfills the Ghost Dance Messiah vision which Black Elk had in 1890. On later reflection, Black Elk recognized the Ghost Dance Messiah as Christ, which became the great mediating symbol between his conscious Catholic life and his repressed Lakota experience. This, perhaps, will restore the "once flowering tree in the center of the nation."[3]

1. Marie Louise von Franz, *Projection and Re-Collection in Jungian Psychology. Reflections of the Soul.* LaSalle and London: Open Court Publishing Co. 1980, p. 83

2. Condensed from Joseph Epes Brown, *The Sacred Pipe: Black Elk's Account of the Seven Rites of the Oglala Sioux.* Norman: University of Oklahoma, 1953, pp. 3-9.

3. One should read the beautiful life of Black Elk in John Neihardt's *Black Elk Speaks: Being the Life Story of a Holy Man of the Oglala Sioux.* Lincoln: University of Nebraska, 1961. One must realize that Neihardt leaves out Black Elk's identification of the Ghost Dance Messiah with Christ. For a complete analysis of this identification one should consult Paul B. Steinmetz, S.J., *Pipe, Bible and Peyote among the Oglala Lakota: A Study in Religious Identity,* Stockholm Studies in Comparative Religion (19) 1980, pp. 154-156

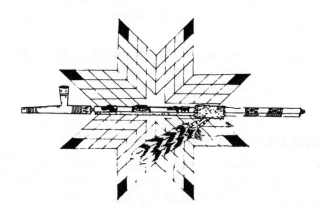

Prayer Before Meditation

I offer the Pipe tonight
although someone else is holding the Pipe.
I offer the Pipe for Hope,
who is in the hospital,
that she will get completely well.
I offer it as a *wicasa wakan*, a holy man.
Last night you respected the power
of the priest,
the power of the sacrament
of the Holy Annointing
by calling the priest.
And Hope is getting better.
Tonight, as a priest
I sit at the same level as you
with great humility
in prayer.
And I respect any good power.
I do wish that we pray to Almighty God.
And so let all of us have the sense of prayer
in our lives all the time.

Paul B. Steinmetz, S.J. at a yuwipe*meeting
conducted by George Plenty Wolf*

Traditional Lakota Spirituality

The Sacred Calf Pipe

My son, Orval,
who is keeper of the Calf Pipe,
unwrapped the Pipe
two years ago.
That was the last time.
Each keeper does this
in order to obtain power
from the ceremony.
When Orval did it,
a thunder storm came up as a sign.

Stanley Looking Horse

Green Grass is a place
where all the spirits
of all the medicine men
who pray through the Pipe
are present
since all their Pipes
are related to the Calf Pipe

Stanley Looking Horse

Two nights ago
drunks came down
and broke into the small house
and left their beer cans
and wine bottles
before the Calf Pipe.
They don't hurt the Calf Pipe
nor the keeper
but they hurt themselves.
Something bad will happen to them
within four years.

Stanley Looking Horse

On the first day of the Green Grass Sun Dance
the Calf Pipe was brought out for a ceremony.
When a complaint was made at my presence,
a tribal leader made it clear
that anybody, regardless of race,
who believed in the Calf Pipe
could be present at the ceremony.
Four saplings were planted in the ground
and a string of tobacco pouches
enclosed the sacred place on four sides
except for an entrance on the northeast.
Frank Fools Crow and Orval Looking Horse
carrying the Calf Pipe bundle,
a buffalo hide, fur side out,
entered the sacred space
and laid it on a bed of sage.
A group of singers around a large drum
sang a Pipe song.
For two hours
the Sun Dancers and the people
entered the sacred place
with their shoes removed
knelt before the Calf Pipe bundle
touching their Pipes to the bundle
and making offerings to the Pipe.

Paul B. Steinmetz, S.J.

The red Pipe bowl is the Indian's blood,
the blood of a woman.
The stem is the breath of a man.
The two together guarantee
the future generations.
If the Pipe is lost,
it will be the end of the Sioux people.

Stanley Looking Horse

In October of 1976
I requested to pray in the presence of the
    Calf Pipe.
Stanley Looking Horse conducted a sweat lodge
    ceremony
and late at night opened the small house
where the Calf Pipe is kept.
I went in and felt overwhelmed by its presence.
He told me that this was the first time
that a priest or minister had made this request
and that he was pleased.
During a later visit
he told me that the Calf Pipe gave its approval
of my visit by four bellowings.
He heard it.
Good things have been happening to him
since I prayed before the Calf Pipe.

Paul B. Steinmetz, S.J.

Traditional Lakota Spirituality

Relation to the Earth
and the Spirit World

I pray with the Pipe
in the four directions.
I pray to the west first
because that is where
the thunders come from mostly.
I pray first to God,
then to the animals
and then to the thunders.
The Pipe received its power from God.
There is no human being
that made this Pipe powerful and holy
but it is from God.

John Iron Rope

We Indians live in a world of symbols and images
where the spiritual and the commonplace are one.
To the white man symbols are just words,
spoken or written in a book.
To us they are a part of nature,
part of ourselves —
the earth, the sun, the wind and the rain,
stones, trees, animals, even little insects
like ants and grasshoppers.
We try to understand them
not with the head
but with the heart,
and we need no more than a hint
to give us the meaning.

John Lame Deer

To the good Mother Earth
we offer you this Pipe
that as we live upon you,
we walk and sit and play,
cry and have pain,
laugh and have joy
on your breasts.
Feed on those things
that make us live,
the food that you produce,
the herbs we need so much
to keep the people healthy.
Bless the streams and the mountains,
the trees, the grass, the shrubs,
all that you put forth from your breasts.
Great Spirit, bless our Mother Earth
so our people may continue to live
in harmony with nature.
And all that the Indian does
with the Sacred Pipe
be blessed also —
the rocks, the buffalo robe,
the skull we use as an altar,
our Sun Dance and our Sun Dance tree.

Pete Catches, Sr.

For us Indians there is just the pipe,
the earth we sit on
and the open sky.
The spirit is everywhere.
Sometimes it shows itself through an animal,
a bird or some trees and hills.
Sometimes it speaks from the Badlands,
a stone, or even from the water.
That smoke from the peace pipe,
it goes straight up to the spirit world.
But this is a two-way thing.
Power flows down to us through that smoke,
through the pipe stem.
You feel that power as you hold your pipe;
it moves from the pipe right into your body.
The pipe is not just a thing,
it is alive.

John Lame Deer

There was a man named Dried Meat.
He killed a deer
for a hungry family.
He told them he was in a bad mood
for having done it.
They laughed at him
and said he was going crazy
and that he was living too much by himself
and that he should move into town.
He called his friends—
ants, spiders, frogs, deer—
and they all surrounded him.
A buffalo appeared on a north bank
kicking up the dust.
The next day
the entire family was found dead.

John Makes Shines

These are the main Lakota spirits:
Wakinyan...a fabled bird,
hidden in the clouds
whose voice is the thunder
and the glance of whose eye is the lightning.
This spirit governs the weather, the clouds,
    and the rain
It may be invoked
and pleased or displeased
and will give good weather or bad as it sees fit.
Mahpiya, the heavens, the clouds, the sky,
a presiding spirit over these
which hears invocations,
is pleased or displeased,
and shows this by giving or withholding
pleasant weather, rains, storms, frosts, and dews
or by hot winds sent as punishment.
Maka, the Earth,
a presiding Spirit of the Earth,
which hears invocations and is pleased
    or displeased
and shows this
by giving good or bad seasons and
by producing plenty or scanty vegetation.
This spirit especially presides over the medicines
that come from the earth
and gives them potencies for good or evil
according to...the methods of the
    medicine man's invocations.
Waziya, a mythical giant at the north
who causes the cold north wind
by blowing from his mouth.

He comes near during the winter
and recedes during the summer
and is in continual contest with the south winds.
He presides over snow and ice....
Wiyohiyanpa, the place where the sun arrives...
the Spirit of the East
which presides over the day.
Okaga, the South,
the Spirit of the South
which...presides over the south winds and
    warm weather
and over the production of fruits and grain.
Wiyohipeyata, the place where the sun retires,
the Spirit of the West
which presides over the evening and the coming
    of darkness
and is present at the death of man and animals.
Tatanka, the Spirit of the Buffalo Bull
which presides over fecundity, virtue, industry,
    and the family.
It also patronizes hunting.
This spirit remains with the skull of the buffalo
and is in continual conflict with the Spirit of
    Coyote.
It is the guardian of young women
and women during their menstrual periods
and during pregnancy.
Mato, the Spirit of the Bear
which presides over love and hate
and bravery and wounds
and many kinds of medicines.
He was the patron of mischief and fun.

Mica, the Spirit of the Coyote
which presides over thieving and cowardice
and all mischief of a malevolent kind.
This spirit was continually trying to outwit
    Tatanka
Sungmanitu, the Spirit of the Wolf
which presided over the chase and war parties.
Sunka, the Spirit of the Dog
presided over friendship and cunning.
Hehaka, the Spirit of the Male Elk
presided over sexual relationship.
Capa, the Spirit of the Beaver
was the patron of work, provision, and of
    domestic faithfulness.
Wambli, the Spirit of the Eagle
presided over councils, hunters, war parties, and
    battles.
Cetan, the Spirit of the Hawk
presided over swiftness and endurance.
Zuzeca, the Spirit of the Snake
presided over the ability to do things slyly,
to go about unknown and unseen, and of lying.
Hnaska, the Spirit of the Frog
was the patron of occult powers.
Hogan, the Spirit of the Fish
was the patron of ablution
and presided over the powers of the waters.
Keya, the Spirit of the Turtle
was the guardian of life and patron of surgery.
Unktomni, the Spider,
presiding genius of pranks and practical jokes
with powers to work magic over persons and
    things.

Thomas Tyon as told to James Walker

From birth to death
we Indians are enfolded in symbols
as in a blanket.
An infant's cradle board is covered with designs
to ensure a happy, healthy life for the child.
The moccasins of the dead
have their soles beaded in a certain way
to ease the journey to the hereafter.
For the same reason most of us have tattoos
on our wrists—
just a name, a few letters, a design.
The Owl Woman who guards the road to the spirit
    lodges
looks at these tattoos and lets us pass.
They are like a passport.
Some Indians believe
that if you don't have these signs on your body,
that Ghost Woman will throw you over a cliff
and you will have to roam the earth
endlessly as a ghost.

John Lame Deer

I'm an Indian.
I think about common things like this pot.
The bubbling water comes from the rain cloud.
It represents the sky.
The fire comes from the sun
which warms us all, men, animals, trees.
The meat stands for the four-legged creatures,
our animal brothers,
who gave of themselves so that we should live.
The steam is living breath.
It was water, now it goes up to the sky,
becomes a cloud again.
These things are sacred.
Looking at that pot full of good soup,
I am thinking how, in this simple manner,
The Great Spirit takes care of me.

John Lame Deer

It is the belief of the Indian people
that to the west
the Great Spirit put holy people
and they are known as thunder beings.
We pray to them
that through their help
the Great Spirit will bring rain
or put it off
according to our needs.
To the north
we pray to the buffalo nation
who adopted the redman
to be his younger brothers.
The buffalo said to him:
"Look at the prairie.
You see all the food
so that I will not be hungry.
So, when you become my little brother,
you will not be hungry.
And look at the fur on the fore part of my body,
so thick and so warm.
In the greatest blizzards
I can face into it and eat grass and live.
And so, little brother, you shall not be cold."
And to the east
is the elk nation,
known for its medicine.
To the south
is the crane nation.
To the Indian people
that direction is the spirit road.
After we leave this world
our spirits travel that way.

Pete Catches, Sr.

36

If we care enough about an animal
its spirit will continue to live.
If we don't,
its spirit won't.
Because of this
the Indians took feathers
from a dead eagle.

Victor Bull Bear

The stone
my husband had on the hill
during his vision quest
is in the drawer.
The spirit of the stone
guards the trailer.

Mary Walks

Listen to the air.
You can hear it, feel it,
smell it, taste it.
Woniya wakan, the holy air,
which renews all by its breath.
Woniya wakan, spirit, life, breath, renewal,
it means all that.
We sit together, don't touch,
but something is there,
we feel it between us,
as a presence.
A good way to start thinking about nature,
talk about it.
Rather talk to it,
talk to the rivers, to the lakes,
to the winds,
as to our relatives.

John Lame Deer

The Indian's symbol is the circle, the hoop.
Nature wants things to be round
The bodies of human beings and animals have no
    corners.
With us the circle stands for the togetherness
of people who sit with one another
around the campfire,
relatives and friends united in peace
while the pipe passes from hand to hand.
The camp in which every tipi had its place
was also in a ring.
The tipi was a ring in which people sat in a circle
and all the families in the village
were in turn circles
within a larger circle,
part of the larger hoop
which was the seven campfires of the Sioux,
representing one nation.
The nation was only part of the universe,
in itself circular and made of the earth,
which is round,
of the sun which is round,
of the stars which are round.
The moon, the horizon, the rainbow—
circles within circles,
with no beginning and no end.

John Lame Deer

Traditional Lakota Spirituality

Spiritual Food

Before an Indian takes a drink of water
and passes it to his people,
he pours some on Mother Earth.
It is an offering of thanksgiving
for the ones
that Mother Earth took back to her bosom
so that these spirit people
can partake of the water.
In spiritual food
the four foods offered
are water, meat, corn and fruit
because they are the only ones
that the Indian had.
One gives a piece of food,
not a big one, nor too small
but just so.
The right amount goes a long way.

Lawrence Hunter

In the Peyote meeting
they take the spiritual food
either to the cemetery
or place it in the fireplace.
If the road man conducts the service
in the right way
without distractions,
you can see the spirits of the deceased
at this time.
Just like in the Bible
after Jesus was crucified,
the apostles were praying in a room at night
and Jesus appeared in the midst of them
in spirit.
Or Jesus appeared to the disciples
on the way to Emmaus.
After He blessed and broke the bread,
He disappeared.
The same thing in the meeting
when you present spiritual food,
the spirits really come around.
Spiritual food reminds me
of the Lord feeding the people with the loaves.
And so, the person who handles the spiritual food
has to be perfect.

Bernard Ice

The road man wanted my boy
to put spiritual food
in the fireplace
during a peyote meeting.
I told the fire man
he was too young to handle that.
When you carry spiritual food,
you have to watch your every step.
From the time you put spiritual food
into the ground
you have to take care of it
in the right way,
not only in the memorial meeting
but for the rest of your life.
So I told the road man
my boy was too young
and I didn't want him to do it.
But he insisted.

So my boy prayed
for the American Indian Movement
and you know what trouble they are in.
And that was overpowering him,
the people he was praying for.
He was too young
to take care of a powerful prayer like that.
It was too dangerous for him.
It would have been good
if he had a strong mind
that could overpower the wicked
and stay in good ways.
And so my boy died.

Beatrice Weasel Bear

Traditional Lakota Spirituality

The Sweat Lodge Ceremony

Before we were born,
we were in the womb of our mother.
Every person came
from the womb of a mother.
We call the earth our Mother Earth
and when the door of the sweat lodge
is closed,
we feel we are reborn
in the womb of our Mother the Earth.
We are there,
the heat, the water, the rocks,
the beginnning of time
and the end of time.

Pete Catches, Sr.

We will sing
the Sun Dance song,
"Great Spirit
have pity on us,"
so that through our suffering
in the sweat lodge
we can pray
for our brothers and sisters
taking part
in the Longest Walk
from San Francisco to Washington, D.C.
to protest the violations
of the treaties,
that the Great Spirit
will encourage and strengthen them.

Selo Black Crow in sweat lodge ceremony

We do not worship creation.
We worship the Great Spirit
in the creation He has made.
We pray to the pail of water
in the sweat lodge
but that represents
all the waters everywhere,
the Great Lakes, the Mississippi, the Missouri,
all the waters in the world.
The pail of water
represents all of that.
We pray through the water
to the Great Spirit.

Pete Catches, Sr.

A medicine man
prepared a sweat lodge for me.
The Pipe was loaded
and then he got scared.
He was also praying for my separated wife
and he was afraid
that the people might consider him
a double-crosser.
However, last night
he cut six pieces of my flesh
which I put in a cloth
and offered to the four directions,
the heavens and Mother Earth.
I asked that no harm would come to me
since the Pipe was loaded
and the ceremony was not finished.

Vincent Black Feather

The concluding sweat lodge allows one
to drink water
and to pray with the Pipe
to complete the ceremony.
The main purpose
is to untie the knot
that connects the person
with the sacred ceremony
so that he can go
from the sacred world to the profane again.
He also has to live
with the responsibility of his vision
and the concluding sweat lodge
allows him to purify himself
for carrying that out.

Richard Moves Camp

Traditional Lakota Spirituality

The Vision Quest

When I was eleven years old,
I had a dream
that I was facing the west
on a hill.
There was lightning.
I looked down
and I was holding a Pipe.
The dream bothered me.
I dreamt it twice in one week.
I went to Sam Moves Camp, Sr.
who put me in a sweat lodge
with water and no food
since I was only eleven years old.
since I was only eleven years old.
When I was fourteen,
Sam put me on the hill
for a vision quest.
I remembered from my Catholic instruction
that Christ fasted.

Richard Moves Camp

In the early morning
there was a deep frost.
I was standing with my Pipe
and the ground was white
and my buffalo robe was white.
I felt the chill.
I dropped the buffalo robe
and stood in my breech cloth
feeling the chill over my whole body.
My Pipe was getting heavier and heavier.
My hands dropped down
and I had to pull them up
over and over.
Then the sun started to come up.
The first rays were on my back.
Then, I turned to the north
and the sun warmed my right side
and to the east
and the rays were right in my face
and to the south
and the rays were right in my face
and to the south
and the rays were on my left side.
And I thanked the Great Spirit
after feeling the chill of the frost
that He warmed me
with the rays of the sun.
It was an experience I will never forget.

Pete Catches, Sr.

Early in the morning
just before the sun came up,
I started praying
and I heard something.
It seemed like someone was coming.
I looked towards the South
and it was the Great Spirit
that was coming
in the form of a skeleton.
He came up to me
so I hit him with my Peace Pipe.
Then I went into a coma
and when I came to,
I was standing with my different colored clothes.
"Did you hear what your great Grandfather
   told you?"
I answered back and said no.
"Everything he told you,
you will not know now
but he will appear
and you will hear everything
he said to you
when you go back to the sweat lodge."
I wondered who it was that said those words.
And I looked around
and I found a bunch of pigeons
that were sitting on a limb
and they were the ones talking to me.

George Plenty Wolf

The spirits will be coming towards you,
singing.
Then all of a sudden
I saw this man who was a skeleton.
He was jumping up and down
and turning himself around.
He told me to recognize him good.
Then he came as close as he possible could.
" Recognize me good.
I am all skin and bones,
full of skeletons.
When a man is sick
and is skin and bones,
if you treat him,
you can restore him to health."
Then I saw four skeletons
in the four directions
and each one of the four colors.
The spirits told me
"When you go to a sick person,
you will say it is impossible
to restore him back to health.
But, always remember what we told you.
When this singing starts,
this man who is a skeleton
will be the one
that will give the treatment.
He will be using those rattles.

When a person is very sick,
some will not believe
he can be restored back to life.
People who visit the sick will be amazed.
Gradually he will be restored back
to live and put on weight."

John Iron Rope

John Fast Wolf was a medicine man.
He made a four-day-and-night- vision quest
because his mother had been very sick
and recovered.
He saw a snake wrapped around himself
at night.
The next day it disappeared.
Also a man, almost skin and bones,
told him to look over in a certain direction
and he saw men
during the night.
The next day
he saw that the men were plants
which he used for medicine.

Vincent Black Feather

In the early dawn
one will hear voices
but he should not be alarmed
and he should pray.
Or he might see a vision
but, whatever is evil
cannot come into the sacred place.
The evil forces are afraid of the Pipe.
The evil forces are tempting him.
Last of all
he will hear some man's voice
that will be telling him comforting words.
The four winds are the ones
that will be talking to him.
He will hear the voices of the four winds
but they will be the same voice.
These are the men
that are good in nature and kind.
The other one is evil.

John Iron Rope

Suddenly, during my vision quest,
I felt an overwhelming presence.
Down there with my in my cramped hole
was a large bird.
He was flying around me
as though he had the whole sky to himself.
I could hear his cries,
sometimes near me, sometimes far, far away.
I felt feathers or a wing touching my back and
     head.
This feeling was so overwhelming
that it was too much for me.
I grasped the rattle
with the forty pieces of my grandmother's flesh
and many little stones,
tiny fossils picked up from the ant heap,
little stones supposed to have power.
I shook my rattle
and it made a soothing sound like rain upon
     a rock,
but it did not calm my fears.
I took the sacred pipe in my hand
and began to sing and pray
"Tunkashila, grandfather spirit, help me."
But this did not help.
I started to cry.
Crying, even my voice was different.
I sounded like an older man.
I couldn't even recognize this strange voice.
In the end I pulled the star quilt over me.

John Lame Deer

I saw a man with a black side and a red side,
braids on the black side
and loose hair on the red.
The braids were wrapped around a red cloth,
the sign of danger.
This meant that prayers would contain any
    danger.
The loose hair was there for sorrow
so that they could wipe their tears
as those who lament in the Sun Dance.
The man wore buckskin leggins, quill work
and three rows of eagle claws around his neck
and was carrying a Pipe.
He had the most beautiful outfit I had ever seen.
The man said:
"When you conduct meetings to heal,
I will be there."

Dawson No Horse

I dreamt of my deceased father
dancing with a buffalo skull
on his head.
He took it off
and offered it to me
and said, "Take it."
Then I woke up.
I am afraid of dreams
because my dreams come true.

Reid Bad Cob

Traditional Lakota Spirituality

The Sun Dance

The center pole
is like God.
Since we cannot see God
with our eyes,
the tree is a reminder of God,
that God is the center of the whole world
of all people.
When you see the center pole,
it is to remind you that God is there.
The tree reminds people to be as one.
The personal offerings of people
are tied to the center pole.

George Plenty Wolf

All the Sun Dancers have a special prayer
but the main one is before the Sun Dance starts.
Each dancer hugs the cottonwood tree
and while hugging it,
he asks the Great Spirit
for strength to lead a good life
for the benefit of the people.
He even cries
to show that he is repentant
of the bad things.
He asks for strength
so that his sacrifice
will be pleasing to the Great Spirit.

Edgar Red Cloud

There are two Pipes
used in the Sun Dance.

One is buried
beneath the Sun Dance pole
and the other is used
to represent all the Sun Dance prayers.
The reason why they buried the one Pipe
is because, while a man is alive,
he can smoke the Pipe,
but after he is dead
he cannot smoke it.
So the buried Pipe
represents a burial place
under the ground.

Edgar Red Cloud

Sun Dance Songs

1.

Great Spirit have pity on me.
I want to live
Therefore I do this.

You Spotted Crow
You Spotted Crow
Pray with the Pipe
   as you will win a war.
(Sung during World War II)

2.

My friend, the Dawn
My friend, the Dawn
The Dawn, come and stand.
(Sung in the early morning)

3.

My friend I am coming.
My friend I am coming.
I come over the earth
   with the entire power.
(Prayer to a spirit)

4.

A man I love
I didn't get to see him.
(A girl's boy friend is in the dance)

5.

Spotted Crow, do you want water?
Do you want water?
Do you want water?
You say it.

Spotted Crow, are you hungry?
Are you hungry?
Are you hungry?
You say it.

(The two songs above are temptation songs)

Sung in Lakota by Edgar Red Cloud

We will not have the same power
until we have the faith of our grandfathers
but we are going that way.
No one will tell you how to pray,
how to live.
You must go to the sacred hoop,
to the tree.
You must prepare yourselves;
you have to find yourselves.
The power you are going to talk to,
you have to do that yourselves.
Come into the sacred hoop.
You have to seek and find yourselves.
There is no other way.
Find God the hard way.
No other religion is so severe and trying
as the Sun Dance Religion
as exercised by our traditional people.
We must understand what they were doing.
We received many blessings
from the Great Spirit.
Everything we receive, even life,
we return in thanksgiving.
We pray to understand the law of nature
which is God.

Matthew King, Sun Dance Speech

The teen-age boy and girl, twins,
who were pierced and tied to the tree
both dreamt
when they were about eight years old,
of hanging from a tree.
Their interpretation was
that they should be pierced together
at a Sun Dance.
That is the reason why
the girl was pierced on the left arm
and the boy on the right side of the chest
and they pulled free together
in a dance
in which they were the only ones pierced.

Selo Black Crow

While a Lakota is being pierced
at the center,
the dancers form a large circle
around the tree,
the ones previously pierced
being part of the circle.
Those dragging buffalo skulls
do so right behind the circle of dancers.
There are four men with their Pipes
always facing the sun
and following its course throughout the day.
After the pierced dancer
embraces the tree for the fourth time,
he runs backward
throwing his weight against the rope
tied to the tree
breaking his flesh to be free,
encouraged by the shouts
of relatives and dancers.

Paul B. Steinmetz, S.J.

During the piercing
which takes place every day,
relatives and friends
stand behind the man pierced
within the sacred place
dancing in rhythm with the drum beat
and shouting encouragement
as he runs back to pull himself free.
Others follow men
pierced in the back
dragging buffalo skulls
around in a circle.
When a dancer was suspended
from the tree,
all the people present were asked to stand up,
remain silent
and pray for success in his efforts.

Paul B. Steinmetz, S.J.

And so ended a ceremony
in which six symbols—
the drum, the eagle whistle, the Pipe,
the tree, the buffalo skull and the sun—
caught the Lakota imagination.
The almost constant beat of the drum,
the eagle whistle blown in unison with it,
the offering of the Sacred Pipe,
the tree which was embraced
as a source of strength
and from which they tore themselves free,
the buffalo skull
placed in a position of honor
on the altar
and dragged in torture
around the sacred circle
and the sun
bright and hot and unmerciful
engulfed the consciousness
of both dancers and spectators alike.

Paul B. Steinmetz, S.J.

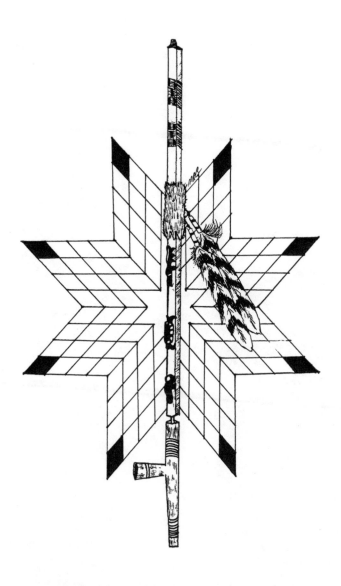

Traditional Lakota Spirituality

Yuwipi **Meetings**

Therefore, I offer this Pipe.
Almighty, Great Spirit,
between this earth and heaven
there are some animal helpers.
All these four winds, these animals
take charge
and on this earth
there are some animals.
All these which watch the earth,
Almighty, Great Spirit,
may they help me with these prayers
for the thing which I ask of You.
God, all these animals are my friends.
That is why I am walking with this Pipe.

George Plenty Wolf in a yuwipi *meeting*

I pray with four songs;
I pray to the four winds.
Great Spirit, look at us.
I pray with the Sacred Pipe.
Have pity on me
as I pray to You
with my Pipe.
Every time I do this,
You make me stronger.
Have pity on me
as I pray with the Sacred Pipe.
Great Spirit, look down upon us.
We need your Help.
Take this Sacred Pipe,
I have done this
to live with my people.
I pray to my Grandfather,
Look at this Sacred Pipe.
Look at this Sacred Pipe.
I am pitiful with my Pipe.
I am pitiful, my Grandfather.
Look at my Sacred Pipe.

Charles Kills Rhee, yuwipi *song*

Great Grandfather,
look at me, here pitiful,
asking for Your help.
I stand here in the center
of Your sacred ground.
Pity me.
I am here with my people
with Your sacred Pipe.
Have pity on all of us,
as we are pitiful.
I have made a road through the clouds
for myself with sacred Pipe.
Great Grandfather, You are coming.
Great Grandfather, You are coming.
We pray for Your forgiveness.
Have pity on us.
Look up at the clouds
as I have made a path
with my sacred Pipe.

George Plenty Wolf in a yuwipi *meeting*

A medicine man's personal medicine
is never revealed.
What is in the medicine is a sort of mystery
even to the medicine man himself.
The power of the medicine man
begins with the medicine bag that he owns.
It shall remain with him
a secret to himself and to the public
for as long as he lives.
When he passes from the world,
he takes this medicine bag with him.

Pete Catches, Sr.

Red Star was conducting a meeting
on a dirt floor
to doctor a girl with tuberculosis.
The girl was inside a circle of war paint
which was painted on the dirt.
Red Star was told by the spirits
that if the spirit helpers missed the circle,
the girl would die,
but if they were within,
she would live.
During the singing
there were vibrations in the ground
and a gopher threw up dirt
out in the middle of the circle.
The gopher came out
and went back into the ground.

Pete Swift Bird

My wife had a stroke on one side of her face.
I took here to a *yuwipi* man to be cured.
He conducted four nights of *yuwipi* meetings.
On the fourth night
during the meeting
a spirit put a stone in her hand.
She closed her hand
until the end of the meeting.
The *yuwipi* man told us to wrap it
in red cloth
and put a blue and yellow ribbon on it.
My wife was cured.
We carry the medicine pouch
in our pickup all the time.
The spirit gave us a song
that we sing on long trips.
The blue ribbon stands for the night,
the yellow for the day.
The song is the following:
   I pray with this.
   I pray with this.
   I pray with this Pipe.
   I send my voice to Grandfather.

Matthew Two Bulls

Yuwipi Songs

1.

Friend, do it like this.
Friend, do it like this.
Friend, do it like this.
When you do this, whatever you ask
    it shall be done.
When you sit inside one sacred place,
Offer tobacco with the Pipe.
When you do this, whatever you ask
    it shall be done.

2.

Your Grandfather is sitting looking down.
Pray to him, pray to him.
He sits there looking down.

3.

Grandfather, come to see me.
Grandfather,come to see me.
So that my relatives and I will live
    I am sending my voice.

4.

From above I come.
From above I come.
My Grandfather told me to come,
    therefore I come.
From above I come.
A people are crying, therefore I come
    from above.

5.

The Thunders come to stop in a circle.
The Thunders come to stop in a circle.
Friend, look upon one person that might be crying.
The Thunders come to stop in a circle.
Friend, look upon one person that might be crying.

6.

Over there they eat a dog.
Over there they eat a dog.
The Thunder People eat a dog
in a holy way.

7.

Friend, go out, go out.
In a holy way go out, go out.

From above looking down I sit;
go out.
From above looking down I sit;
go out.

Sung in Lakota by Lawrence Hunter

Native American Church

The Altar

In the Cross Fire Fireplace
they use the star.
Jesus Christ,
the offspring of David,
is the Morning Star.
When Jesus was born,
the three Magi followed the star.
Maybe someone wants to be reborn again.

Bernard Ice

The Half Moon altar is the path of life.
Many people have gone on the path
of this life and beyond.
The mound is Mother Earth,
where you come from
and you are going back in there.
It is the same as the Bible passage,
"from dust to dust."
As you sit and eat Peyote,
the altar becomes a grave
into which many a man has gone.
People use different symbols in the ashes,
like the eagle which is the symbol of courage.
Because the water bird is timid,
innocent and pure,
they use it as a symbol to cure a person
who is really sick.
They use sand instead of earth
because the sand is not the symbol
of the grave like the earth is.
They use the sand
because they want the person to get well
and not die.

Lawrence Hunter

I often wondered
why the moon was on the altar.
It could have been something else.
In the beginning
Adam and Eve were in the garden of paradise.
They disobeyed God's commandment
and hid themselves.
They thought that the sun was light.
But, the moon is there also.
They can't hide from God
since night or day He has His light.
The moon shining
even when Adam and Eve sinned
is one of the reasons
why the Half Moon Fireplace
is open to everybody, even sinners.
The moon is just like life;
new moon, quarter moon and then full
just as we grow up.
Then as we grow old,
the moon also diminishes.
Then, they put a mark on the moon altar
which is the road of life.

Sometimes the road man makes four marks
across the road of life.
These stand for the four directions
and for the four stages of life.
The white man spent a lot of money
going to the moon.
Here we have it right here on our altar.

Bernard Ice

Joe Sierra introduced new designs
into the Half Moon Fireplace.
all connected with servicemen.
He knew this by eating the medicine
and praying.
He put the triangle there
which stands for the three Persons in one God
but also, when a serviceman returns home dead,
the flag is folded into a triangle
and given to the relatives.
At midnight he put the heart there
representing the Sacred Heart of Jesus
as well as the purple heart
given to servicemen for brave deeds.
At the main smoke he put the star
for Jesus, the Morning Star
and for the gold star
given to mothers who lose a son in war.
Finally the eagle,
which is the king of all the birds
and closest to the Almighty
and also the emblem that servicemen wear.

Beatrice Weasel Bear

In the Half Moon
the main ash design is the bird,
either an eagle, dove or water bird.

The eagle is the king of all birds.
He flies higher than any other bird.
The eagle represents the Great Spirit
since He is the highest.
When you see a marshall or FBI person,
he is wearing a badge with the eagle.
The person with the eagle on him
is somebody that you have to show respect
    towards.
It is the national bird.
Somebody shot an eagle
and it cost him $5,000.
When Congress passes a law,
they put the seal of an eagle on it.
So, in a meeting
when all the prayers and singing
have been completed,
they put the eagle in the fireplace.
God approves of the prayers
since the seal is right there on the altar.

Again it is a dove.
John baptized Jesus in the River Jordan
and a dove descended on Him.
Through that Jesus contacted the Spirit.

The water bird
represents the Holy Spirit.
The waterbird flies above the lakes
and when he sees something to eat,
he can dive into the water.
If he sees a sinner,
that could be represented by a fish.
Or it might be a human
that is suffering and needs help.
He could get him even out of the water.

Bernard Ice

Native American Church

The Water Drum

Sometimes I am sitting here at home
all alone.
But I am not alone.
I have a drum, water, gourd rattle.
I sing the songs
and my worries are gone.
I feel good again
and refreshed.

Bernard Ice

When you beat the drum,
it brings out the sounds
that represent the Thunders.
It will go a long way
through the valley and canyons.
So, by using it
the sound goes up to the Almighty.
Since it goes along the horizon,
it must go up too.
Because the Thunders are a source of rain,
they put water in the drum.
For the first man who tied the drum
there must have been a blessing on him
because it has the crown on the top
and the star on the bottom.
The Thunder brings the water
and it brings the Son, Jesus.

Bernard Red Cloud

The drum has seven stones
which stand for
the seven Indian sacraments
and the seven sacraments of the Catholic Church.
The seven Indian sacraments are:
Peyote, the dirt Half Moon, fire, water,
corn, meat and fruit.
The thong on the top represents
the crown of thorns that Jesus wore.
The skin on the drum is the animal hide
used for clothing.
Jesus wore a robe in the passion.
The soldiers took it away
and gambled for it.
This is a sign of the evil forces
which are about.
Jesus' hands were tied with a rope
when He was in custody.
Everything is in the Bible.

Bernard Ice

The drum has water in it
like Mother Earth.
The star on the bottom of the drum
is the Morning Star.
"One day He will come from the east
and He wants me to prepare to meet Him."
That's a morning water song.
Jesus says, "I am the bright Morning Star."
And so, as we behold Him,
we ask Jesus
that we have life everlasting and peace.
As you beat the drum,
the sound goes south
to the land of the spirits
and to those who are there.
Some are drummers, some road men,
Some fire men, some cedar men,
people who were in meetings, singers.
The echo of this drum
brings the spirits back
so that they can partake of the meeting
and listen
because they will be remembered in the prayers.
Through the spirits we can get a blessing.

Lawrence Hunter

The drummer for this meeting was late
and was unable to tie his own drum.
He didn't like the way the drum was tied,
so he took it apart during the meeting
to retie it,
which is against the regulations.
One person defended him
when objections were raised.
But just like the drum
both families were torn apart.
The drummer began living with a woman
married to his own brother
and the one who defended him
was separated from his wife for a while.
I don't believe in superstitions
but that happened.

Emerson Spider

Native American Church

The Morning Water Woman

I had a vision of the morning water.
I saw the big dipper.
When the handle is up
and the dipper part down,
it is the morning water time,
when the woman brings in the water.
At that time the dipper is tilted over
and the water drips out
and hits the clouds.
It lightnings
and the water comes through
in a shower
and hits the mountains and hills.
Streams start flowing down to the creek.
The water woman comes up to the creek
and gets water in a bucket.
She was facing east in my vision
with her hands lifted up in prayer.
She got the water
that came from the dipper
and took it into the tipi
and blessed it.
I saw it come from the big dipper.

Bernard Ice

The Morning Water Woman
is like Mother Earth.
She is mother of all.
From her bosom came the water.
She gave all her children
the plants
and the various species of animals
from the tiniest ant
to the biggest elephant
and the eagle.
The woman who nurses a baby
is just like Mother Earth,
giving to it
so that it will go out into the world
strong and steady.
When the woman brings in the morning water,
she asks God's blessings on all,
that everyone drinks it,
the good and the bad,
that they drink it
because they are her children.
She prays for everyone
who is going to drink the water,
first in the meeting
and then in the whole world.
God gave her the privilege
to pray for everyone,
no matter where they are at,
in conflict or at peace.

Anyone who drinks the water
will remember where it comes from.
The woman is the symbol of Mother Earth.
They call her the Morning Water Woman
and she is mother of all.
If your mother is gone,
she is just like your mother.
Or, if your mother is still living,
you have a second mother.
You came from a mother
and to a mother you shall return.

Lawrence Hunter

Native American Church

Peyote Visions

When you take Peyote,
you have an inner eye
that clears up,
that tells you
what is right and wrong.

Joe American Horse

Tom Bullman got seriously sick one time.
They took him to a meeting
and he took medicine.
They were singing and praying
and towards morning
all at once he saw a vision.
He saw a log house just about to fall over.
But it was braced with logs.
He went into the house
and it was all messed up inside.
He started to clean it up
and he noticed someone was helping him.
Pretty soon they pushed all the trash out.
He came to and
he saw that the house was himself.
The sickness was about ready to get him down
and make him fall over.
The logs bracing the house were prayers
that were said for him.
The man that helped him sweep it out
was the Peyote.
It cleaned him out
and that morning he was well.

Emerson Spider

A woman became sick
and finally unconscious
during a Peyote meeting.
We prayed for her.
The staff made one complete round
and, then, her brother came in and sang.
At that moment she tried to grab something.
I put cedar on the fire
and fanned her with an eagle feather.
Later, she told me her vision.
She prayed that she would take on herself
all the sins of the people at the meeting,
even if she would have to die.
They were all sinful
and so, it happened.
She saw an eagle.
She wanted help
and the eagle didn't look at her
but the other way.
She was in darkness too.
She saw a small hole
that she could go through
but she could not find her way to it.

When her brother was singing,
there was a little feather
floating for that little hole.
Her brother was singing
and he was a little boy
and he was sinless.
His voice represented that little feather
that showed her the way out.
So, she was able to grab the eagle's legs
and he took her out through the hole.

Emerson Spider

My father was sick
and had this vision.
There was a river
that he wanted to get across
and he was looking for a place to cross it.
Then, he saw a man coming towards him,
wearing what looked like a dark suit.
But, as he came close
he saw that it was his skin
which was all black and shrivelled up.
He thought the man had been smiling.
But close up, his mouth was all peeled.
He looked at the man
and saw that it was himself.
He looked at himself
and saw that he had good clothes
and a home
but it was his soul.
His soul was going to determine
whether he was going to live or die.
His sickness was from his soul.

Joe American Horse

I had a vision of being inside the drum
that I was beating.
Every time I beat it,
it looked like the water was coming up.
I wanted to get out but I couldn't.
As I beat it slow,
the water kept going down
but I still couldn't get away from it.
The last song I remember was the chief song.
As I sang it,
God knew I was in this state.
I kept muttering to myself:
"Great Spirit, have pity on me."
As I was drumming,
I kept saying that all the time.
And as I looked at the Chief Peyote,
he was just like a little old man,
wrinkled up, stringy grey hair, barefooted.
He was sitting on the mound.
I couldn't get past him.
He just sat there and looked at me.
And I couldn't hide anything
that came to my mind
because he knew it all.
And I got singing and I came out of it.
The only thing he told me:
"Try to do it right.
If you don't,
you are going to
hurt yourself
and somebody else too."

Lawrence Hunter

At the death of my daughter
different people talked to me.
"You have the instruments
and you belong to the Native American Church.
Now the Almighty wants to know
if you mean business.
So he took one of your children
to see how you are.
Are you going to believe Him or not?
The Almighty took one of yours
and put a seed in heaven,
one of your own blood.
Are you going to believe Him or not?
It's up to you
The Almighty took one of yours
you will get blessings.
He took that nice looking girl
and put her up there
so that your whole family could think about that
and get up there.
The girl made a road for you.
It's all made for you.
She prepared the way."

Bernard Red Cloud

Joe Sierra had tuberculosis real bad.
The hospital said he was going to die.
They gave him a lot of medicine
and he had a vision.
He was wandering off in some desert.
Somebody told him to pray
to his grandfather.
At first, he thought of his natural grandfather.
But the voice kept on repeating:
"Remember your grandfather."
Then, he thought of his great grandfathers
and other grandfathers in an Indian way.
But, he kept on hearing the voice.
Then, all of a sudden it dawned on him
what the voice was saying
and he prayed
to Grandfather, the Great Spirit
and he came out of it
and got well.

Beatrice Weasel Bear

There was the Half Moon,
then a space, the fire,
the water bird ashes
and the tail further on down.
When I looked at that
I saw the Half Moon
and the Peyote sitting on top,
way up there.
It looked real smooth and nice up there.
The Peyote was way up on top like a crown.
In between I saw a dark abyss.
The body of the water bird
was shining and sparkling.
That was a real shiny city.
When I looked there,
I saw a lot of evil things going on there.
Further on down
where the tail part was,
I saw human skulls and bones
covered with snakes.
I thought that if a person stays on top,
he will be all right.
But, if he falls down into the abyss,
and into the city,
he will end up with the bones and snakes.

If a person doesn't follow
the Peyote Road
and goes down into the wicked city,
he will end up with the skeletons.
That's real death, real death.
That's where all the snakes were going
in between the skeletons,
crawling all over them.

Beatrice Weasel Bear

I started singing
but somehow the song was different.
It made me wander around
in some hills
as I closed my eyes.
I was looking for something
that I could not find.
So I cut the song off
and started the second one.
I kept going like that
and I couldn't find
what I was looking for.
I opened my eyes
and I saw that I was making the people restless.
I started the last song
and I found the thing I was looking for.
It was a root.
I picked it up
and put it into my mouth
and started chewing it
and I stuck a piece in my pocket.
About that time
the drum beat came out right
and the roadman started blowing his whistle
and started yelling, "heya, heya."

Everybody started flapping their fans.
The girl's mother came over
and grasped me and said, "Thank you.
As you sang the last song
my little girl came to the door
and she was well."
After the meeting,
they went to the hospital
and brought back the girl well.

Lawrence Hunter

One time I had a gourd
but I didn't have any rocks in it.
I was sitting at a meeting
and thinking about it.
Then, in a vision I saw a gourd
laying on its side
with little rocks coming out of it,
two or three inches thick,
just the size I wanted.
When I looked up,
there was a road going up.
As I walked
the rocks were getting better,
like agates, then like marble, pearls
and finally silver and gold.
They turned out to be diamonds
way up in the sky.
The instruments can help you have a vision
of the good road to heaven.
Even those little rocks can do this.
A vision like that helps
because it gets your mind on heaven,
or on the road of life.
Then, it always leads to prayer.
It made me feel real happy.
I was thankful
that I needed some rocks for my gourd
and it made me see that good road.
Maybe, someday
I will have diamonds in my gourd
when I get up to heaven.

Bernard Ice

Native American Church

Eschatological Reflections

There is a Peyote tone
which comes from
the drum, gourd, whistle and voice
all coming together in the right way.
This Peyote tone
can heal a person.
The trumpets blown by the angels
at the four directions
at the end of the world
will sound like this Peyote tone.

Bernard Ice

The four angels
in the four directions
are waiting.
They are going to blow their whistles,
the ones used in Peyote meetings.
When they do,
they will drop that one bomb
and it is going down into the hole
and the fire that is down there
will ignite
and crack open the earth.

Beatrice Weasel Bear

Just like the Peace Pipe
brought the Indian people together
to pray
so does the Peyote.
The Sioux used to have many enemies.
But, now they use Peyote
to make friends and relations.
When all the tribes use the Peyote,
it will be the end of the world.
Even the Mohawks in New York
use the medicine.
They want my husband, Johnny,
to conduct a meeting over there.

Beatrice Weasel Bear

Both a Pipe and a Peyote meeting
has to go on and on
until you find the perfect meeting.
And that will be the second coming of Christ.
So a meeting is never complete
until you have the perfect meeting
and that is the end.
That is the reason
why one should not be artistic
in building the fire
in a Peyote meeting.
A fire should build itself.
When that day comes,
the Blessed Saviour will say "thank you"
and call us.

Lawrence Hunter

So I want to tell you
about the happy tipi and the sad tipi
to make the children understand this.
Every little child wants to be
in the happy tipi
and not in the sad one.
You could say heaven and purgatory.
There is an old lady
half way through the Milky Way
and she is very old.
She has a little boy with her
and he teaches you.
The little boy can play
with black, red, yellow and white people
without any prejudice in his heart.
But, if the old lady meets you half way,
she will push you off the Milky Way
into the sad tipi
where you have to wait
to meet the Creator.

Selo Black Crow

The Christian Influence

Just like there was a flood
in the Bible
and Noah was saved,
so there was a flood
in the Indian tradition.
A young girl was taken by an eagle
to the highest tree.
When the flood went down,
the eagle took her down from the tree
and turned into a man
and married her.
She had twin boys.

Richard Moves Camp

When the Indians knew Mother Earth,
they knew the Blessed Virgin Mary
but they did not know her by name.
The Woman
who brought the Calf Pipe
is the Blessed Virgin Mary
who brought Christ.

Edgar Red Cloud

Inyan Wasicun Wakan,
the Holy White Stone Man,
that's what we call Moses.
He appeals to us.
He goes up all alone
to the top of the mountain
like an Indian,
to have his vision,
be all alone with his God,
who talks to him through fire, bushes and rocks.
Moses coming back from the hill
carrying stone tablets
with things scratched on them,
he would have made a good Indian medicine man.

John Lame Deer

My grandfather translated the obligation
of a Lakota dream
into Christian terms.
He dreamt of the Thunder.
But he was a Christian man.
So, whenever it thundered,
he took out his Bible
and read it
to fulfill his Lakota dream.

Matthew Two Bulls

The equivalent of Christian sin
in the Indian traditional sense
is breaking one's commitment to the Pipe.
When one prays with the Pipe,
he is obliged to do it in a good way,
not for evil purposes.
The Pipe brings harmony
between men
when they smoke it.
You can't lie through the Pipe.
To go against these things is a sin.

Richard Moves Camp

In October of 1965
the night before the funeral
of Rex Long Visitor
I was seized emotionally
by an inspiration of a ceremony
symbolic of death and resurrection.
And so, on the day of the funeral,
I held a Pipe filled with tobacco
and taking the stem and bowl apart,
I said: "Remember, man,
that the Pipe of your life
some day will be broken."
I then laid the separated Pipe on the coffin.
After the ritual prayers
I took up the separated pieces
and putting them together
I said: "Through the Resurrection of Christ
the life of Rex Long Visitor
and all of us
will be brought together
into eternal happiness."
Then in the four directions I prayed:
"I am the Living and Eternal Pipe,
the Resurrection and the Life;
whoever believes in Me and dies, shall live
and whoever lives and believes in Me
shall never suffer eternal death."
After the fourth direction,
I touched the bowl of the Pipe to the earth
in silence.

Paul B. Steinmetz, S.J.

I was in Rome as a pilgrim
during the Holy Year
and while there I asked the Holy Father
to grant a special Papal Blessing
to the Native American Church.
Pope Paul is the highest representative
of Christ on earth
and he stands in a very special position
between man and Almighty God.
His blessings are very powerful.
There is a picture of Pope Paul
and the four Basilicas in Rome
on the document.
These are Churches of special grace.
I prayed for the Native American Church
in these special places.
The thought struck me
that one prays in the four directions
even in the center of Christianity.
And so, the document reads:
"Most Holy Father,
Rev. Paul Steinmetz, S.J.
humbly begs
for the Native American Church
on the Pine Ridge Reservation
a special Apostolic Blessing."
Then, there is in Latin:

"In the year of Our Lord
the Pope has granted this Apostolic Blessing
in the City of Rome
on June 16, 1975."
Signed by an archbishop.
And when everyone in this tipi
is departed into the next world,
we hope that it will still be preserved
in this Church.
So, I present this great blessing
from Christ through his visible head
as my little gratitude
for everything the Native American Church
has done for me.

*Paul B. Steinmetz, S.J. at the memorial meeting
for Beatrice Weasel Bear's son*

Father Steinmetz
prayed with the Sacred Pipe
for the first time
at my father's funeral.
He presented the Papal Blessing
for the Native American Church
at the memorial meeting for my son.
During that night
as I looked at the Papal Blessing
I realized that I had lost a son
but had gained a Blessing for the Church.
He blessed my son's grace
through the Papal Blessing,
the Sacred Pipe
and the Chief Peyote.
Only the Almighty could bring
these three together.
And it all happened right here
in the same place.
So, I knew my son was in a good place.

Beatrice Weasel Bear

I am glad that Father is interested
in the Pipe.
I would like to have Father
use the Pipe when he prays at Mass.
In a mysterious way
God will give him many privileges.
I know that what Father asks in the Mass,
it will come true.
That's certain.
So, he should take up the Pipe
without any hesitation.

John Iron Rope

I pray with the Pipe
in memory of my vision
just as the priest
changes bread and wine
into the Body and Blood of Christ
in memory of the Last Supper.

Pete Catches, Sr.

The rawhide effigy of the man
hanging from the Sun Dance tree
represents the return of Christ.
That of the buffalo is the Old Testament
and the man is the New Testament.
The piercing of the flesh
is a reminder of the piercing of Jesus.
When the dancers pierce their backs
to drag the buffalo skulls,
Fr. Beuchel (an early missionary) said
that Jesus carried his cross like that.
The man who brought the Sun Dance
from Montana to the Lakota said that
"He was doing something like Noah did,
bringing his people on a certain boat.
We are going through the Sun Dance
and are reaching our destination
just like Noah reached his."

George Plenty Wolf

In later years
piercing in the back near the shoulders
was like carrying the cross.
That is why they did it, then.
Unknown to them
they were practicing that
until Christianity came
and they realized
it meant carrying the cross.
They had no answer for the connection,
only that the true vision
of the medicine man
inspired them to do this.

Edgar Red Cloud

Mass was celebrated in 1969
on the Sun Dance grounds
following the piercing ceremony
after the flags in the four directions
had been removed.
Edgar Red Cloud,
the leader of the Sun Dance singers
sang a Sun Dance song
holding the Sacred Pipe
during the distribution of Holy Communion.
Frank Fools Crow
who performed the piercing
a short time before
received Holy Communion
with Edgar Red Cloud and George Plenty Wolf.

Paul B. Steinmetz, S.J.

This evening we have the heart
as the ash formation in the fireplace.
The Sacred Heart of Jesus Christ.
Coming to Mother's Day.
Even the Lord
when He was crucified,
He looked down upon His mother.
His mother was standing below Him.
He didn't say anything to her.
All He could do was to shed tears.
He cried.
That's all He could do.
So His mother was standing below
and looking up at Him.
There was nothing she could do
to help her Son.
There was nothing she could do.
So the Lord gave Himself for the people
that are here on earth,
not only across the ocean
but over here too,
for the Indian people.
He gave His life for you.
The Great Spirit so loved the world
that He died for you.

John Weasel Bear
from a midnight water talk
at a Mother's Day meeting

I chose to wear red vestments
at the funeral Mass of George Plenty Wolf
because red is the sacred color of power.
And we are celebrating the life of a man
who experienced power,
the power of the Sacred Pipe,
the power of Jesus Christ.
He knew and believed in both powers.
And so, we celebrate with red vestments,
with the sacred color of power.
As Christ was annointed
in the baptism in the Jordan,
so George was annointed
with the Holy Spirit and power
in the visions of his Lakota tradition.
Even when misunderstood by the Church
        he loved,
George had the patience and understanding
to accept this
and to work in his own life
towards bringing the two traditions
together in harmony.
George had the vision
that the gift of the Sacred Pipe
should be brought to the feet of Christ
and laid there
since He is Lord of the Lakota people.
George looked towards the hill
and he saw a man with the Sacred Pipe
fasting and receiving a vision.
And as he kept looking up the hill
suddenly the man with the Sacred Pipe
changed into Christ hanging on the cross.

In carrying the Sacred Pipe
George carried the burdens of many people.
When his spirit left this world,
there were many spirits
of the people he prayed for
with the Sacred Pipe
waiting to receive him.

Paul B. Steinmetz, S.J.
from the homily of the funeral Mass

My grandmother wanted her Last Sacraments.
They were going to call an Episcopal minister
but she said that she wanted them
in the Peyote Way.
William Black Bear gave her four Peyote balls
and my father sang four songs.
They said the Lord's Prayer
and she said "Amen"
and breathed her last breath.

Eva Gap

During most of my life
I was in doubt
about the relation between the Pipe and Christ.
When I believed in the Pipe,
was I betraying myself as a Christian?
What was the meaning in my life
of interpreting my father's life
to John Neihardt and Joseph Brown?
But now that I see
that the Pipe and Christ
are really one,
the doubts of conscience
of many years are ended
and I have a deep spiritual peace
in my soul.
(And that night the vision of the Pipe
leading the Lakota to Christ which we
shared in his log cabin made a deep
impression on both of us.)

Benjamin Black Elk in conversation with the author

A man around 91 years old
and living at Green Grass
told me that
after the Buffalo Calf Woman brought the Pipe,
a white man came
dressed in a buffalo robe
speaking Lakota
and blessed the Pipe.
This was Christ
Who came in the spirit
before the white men brought Him.
I believe that this was Christ
coming in the Spirit to the Indian people
at the same time
that He was born among the white man.
This vision is the reason
why I respect all the Christian Churches.

Richard Moves Camp

OTHER BOOKS IN THE
MEDITATIONS WITH™
SERIES

HILDEGARD of BINGEN
MEISTER ECKHART
MECHTILD of MAGDEBURG
JULIAN OF NORWICH

TM

BEAR & COMPANY, INC.
PO Drawer 2860
Santa Fe, NM 87504